PG-13

A GUIDE TO STRENGTHENING THE
MOTHER-DAUGHTER BOND

ARUNA KRISHNAN

KAAMYA KRISHNAN

COPYRIGHT © 2022 By Aruna Krishnan

All Rights Reserved. This book or any portion thereof may not be reproduced or used in any manner whatsoever without the express written permission of the publisher except for the use of brief quotations in a book review.

This book is dedicated to all moms raising daughters.

Empower them early.
Encourage them often.
Enable them to soar!

*"My mom is a strong-willed lady.
She taught me to believe in myself no matter what anybody else said."*

-Tracey Edmonds

CONTENTS

Preface ix

Prologue 1
I - TATTOOS 3
II - CURFEWS 13
III - MONEY & SPENDING 23
IV - SCREEN TIME 33
V - CLOTHING 43
VI - AFTER HIGH SCHOOL 55
VII - COMMUNICATION 65
VIII - SOCIAL MEDIA 75
IX - MENTAL WELL-BEING 85
X - SOCIAL LIFE 97
Epilogue 109

Closing Credits 111
About The Authors 113
Other Books By Aruna Krishnan 117
A Note From The Authors 119

PREFACE

BY ARUNA KRISHNAN

I remember the day my daughter was born. She was a tiny 5 lb. 14 oz baby! She looked so frail and delicate. When the nurse laid her against my chest and her tiny eyes locked on mine, she sucked on three of her little fingers and just stared at me. That special moment is stored forever in my mind as a cherished memory.

She has grown into a smart, independent, mature young lady. I am so proud of her. She has gone through a lot to get to where she is, and she continues to grow as a person. I do my best to support her through her journey... especially in her teen years.

The teenage years have been interesting, fun, and challenging at times. At the end of the day, I have a bond with her like no other.

Parenting is a journey, and every stage comes with new things to deal with. It's a learning process for sure. I have learned

PREFACE

from both my teens about what works and what doesn't, which is why I am passionate about sharing this book. I hope other mothers with daughters will look at some common topics, see the other side, and better understand each other as a result.

PROLOGUE

The key ingredient to a good relationship is communication. What makes a good communicator?

1. The ability to express your point of view.
2. The ability to actively listen to others.
3. The ability to provide feedback based on verbal and non-verbal cues.

It is very easy to get lost in our perspective, but our willingness to listen to different views helps us be more empathetic toward others. That empathy is what ultimately betters a relationship.

We use three perspectives in this book.

The Mom - By Aruna (Ah-Roo-Nah) Krishnan

First, she shares her experiences of thirty years ago when she was a teenager to show how they influenced her opinions on certain topics.

For each topic, she gets into how she approaches things with her daughter and lays out her concerns and rationale for her stances.

The Daughter - By Kaamya (Kahm-yah) Krishnan

She shares her views, influences, and experiences on the subjects based on what she is currently going through as a teen.

The Narrator - Objective views and conclusions

The narrator provides the independent voice to this story and shares both the worldly view and the path to reconciliation for mom and daughter. The narrator also concludes each chapter with prompts to facilitate dialogue between mom and daughter.

Aruna and Kaamya have enjoyed learning about each other's angles on the topics presented in the book and hope it helps you strengthen your mom-daughter bond.

I - TATTOOS

ARUNA AND KAAMYA KRISHNAN

TATTOOS

ACT 1 - SCENE 1

30 YEARS AGO

Mom reminisces about the perception of tattoos 30 years ago (when she was a teen).

MOM

When I was in Botswana, I did not see many tattoo parlors. Although the tattoo culture had a presence, especially within certain tribes in Africa, it was not a big part of the mainstream culture at the time.

In India, it was an accepted part of the culture, especially among the older generation. My mom got a tattoo when she was twelve years old... without her mom's consent! What is considered "cool" today was nothing more than tradition with varying symbolic representations across the regions in India.

The tattoos were usually in the form of inter-woven, decorative patterns that were intricate yet simple. As a result, I never formed an opinion on tattoos, one way or the other. They seemed harmless enough. At a societal level, Indian culture was accepting of tattoos, so I thought of them as "normal" too.

ACT 1 - SCENE 2

WORLDLY VIEW

NARRATOR

The perception of tattoos has shifted from tradition to rebellion to expression.

About twenty years ago, tattoos were still seen as some form of "non-conformity" and associated with specific groups of people such as bikers, athletes, or misguided teens. Tattoos were frowned upon in a corporate setting. They either prevented people from being hired or gave people a sense of being an outcast in that environment.

Today, tattoos are much more widely accepted. Tattoo artists and their work are highly recognized and celebrated. Corporate America has also progressed a little. Tattoos do not prevent people from being hired, and people are appreciated more for the work they do and the value they bring to the table.

ACT 2 - SCENE 1

TODAY

Mom shares her evolving views on tattoos.

MOM

I admire tattoos that are done very well. It is art at the end of the day.

Up until this past year, I didn't have the desire to get a tattoo. The relative permanency of a tattoo and the fact that its form will not be preserved over time was also a deterring factor for me.

My daughter, on the other hand, has been expressing interest in getting a tattoo for the last few years. I was never opposed to it but just wanted to make sure she thought through the implications of getting the tattoo:

- Will it impede her from getting certain opportunities?
- Will she be fine with it 20 years from now?
- Does it represent something important to her?
- Is she 100% sure she will not have regrets after getting it?

When she turned 18, she asked if I would be willing to get matching tattoos with her. The tattoos would represent her journey of growth and resilience. Something we experienced together... the ups *and* the downs. This journey brought us closer together so marking the journey with matching tattoos felt right.

ACT 2 - SCENE 2

Daughter talks about tattoos in the context of artistic expression and sentimental value.

DAUGHTER

In my opinion, the best part about tattoos is that they can be anything you want them to be and can hold as much significance as you want them to have or none at all.

Parents who don't want their kids to get tattoos may mainly express their concerns surrounding the appearance of tattoos and how other people (such as employers) may perceive them. It's not always an automatic "no" from employers if a potential candidate for a job has tattoos, and I think this way of perceiving tattoos is very outdated.

I see beauty in being able to create art on your body with a story behind it. Impulsiveness may definitely play a factor in wanting to get a tattoo for a change, but then again, if you're sitting in the tattoo chair and realize it's not what you want to do, the worst-case scenario is leaving the tattoo parlor and disappointing a tattoo artist (hopefully it won't have to come to that).

I remember my initial interest in getting a tattoo came about in high school after seeing gorgeous tattoo art online. I started coming up with my own ideas too. I constantly asked my mom if I could get one before I was 18 even though that would mean going to a different state where that was legal for a minor. My mom refused for a while because she expressed worries about the way tattoos would age on my body and how they might only look good for a short period of my life, or that I would regret them when I was older. To put it into perspective and to counter that argument of hers, I see it like this: when I grow old, my body is going to age with me. So, if the tattoos on my body are the WORST looking part of me, I must have aged well! The rest of my body is going to age regardless, so why not enjoy myself when I'm young and indulge in art that can be meaningful to me and represent moments from my life?

When I finally convinced her to get a matching tattoo with me for my 18th birthday, I ended up getting two tattoos! Both hold significant meaning to me and they are small and discreet, which was a personal preference.

ACT 3 - SCENE 1

BRINGING IT TOGETHER

NARRATOR

Start the conversation

Use these conversation starters to understand where both of you stand on the topic of tattoos.

Daughter to Mom

- What concerns you about getting a tattoo?
- Is it a personal belief?
- Is it a fear of not conforming?
- Is it due to concerns for your health?
- Is it because of views that existed when you were a teen?

Mom to Daughter

- Why is it so important to you?
- Are you willing to wait a few months/years before you make the final decision (since this allows her to change her mind)?

II - CURFEWS

ARUNA AND KAAMYA KRISHNAN

CURFEWS

ACT 1 - SCENE 1

30 YEARS AGO

Mom recalls the simplicity of life and the curfews she had to deal with as a teen.

MOM

My parents were lucky that the minimum age for a driver's permit was 18! For most of my teen years, my dad dropped me off and picked me up from friends' parties. Parents did not have to deal with as much uncertainty and fear for their kids' safety as parents experience today.

Eventually, when my friends and I could drive places, our parents understood that we were mature enough to take care of ourselves and make good decisions. They had two rules:

1. Go out in a group.

2. Come back home by 11 PM.

Back to the present.

These rules aren't too far off from the expectation of parents of teens today. In some ways, the worries start sooner... by the time they turn sixteen. It's almost as though this is a written rule in the "Circle of Life." Parents must go through these pangs, learn to deal with them, and finally be fine with letting go. A hard but inevitable process.

ACT 1 - SCENE 2

WORLDLY VIEW

NARRATOR

Curfews exist at many different levels:

1. Household
2. City
3. County
4. State

Curfews help monitor and predict the activity in its respective realm. They are usually intended to keep people safe in the event of emergencies or crises.

City curfews keep residents safe by requiring them to be off the streets by a certain time to minimize the activity (good or bad) in that residential area.

Parental curfews have the same intent. Parents want their kids home by a certain time to ensure they are safe and not exposed to dangers that are more likely to occur later at night such as drunk driving or being negatively approached by strangers.

Those who must abide by curfews tend to feel restricted. Although the intent behind a curfew is good, those impacted by it may not always view it as such whether it is at a household level or a city level.

ACT 2 - SCENE 1

TODAY

Mom shares the challenges around curfews and teens.

MOM

My first exposure to enforcing a curfew was with my son when his friends started driving and he rode with them. I must admit I am glad that my son didn't necessarily have a sense of urgency when it came to getting his license. That conveniently postponed the dread that comes with your first child driving by himself... especially at night. Thank goodness for phone GPS locators!

I faced a similar situation with my daughter. When her friends drove her places, the curfew I set for her was often overridden because her friends' curfew expectations were different. It was very hard to get adherence when I wasn't aligned with her peers' parents.

The curfew came from a place of concern and care, but many times it was perceived as a matter of control or a lack of trust. Although this was not the case, the conclusion that I was being unreasonable, or a worrywart, seemed to be my teen's perception. Once she started driving independently, it became more of a negotiation affair. Curfew vs. counter curfew. It also boiled down to mutual respect and understanding.

ACT 2 - SCENE 2

Daughter's view on curfews, safety measures, and mom's paranoia.

DAUGHTER

First, I should start by saying that I completely understand where my mom's worries stem from when it comes to staying out late at night and what time I should be back home. I watched my mom navigate her way through enforcing reasonable curfews with my older brother and knew that the same situation would apply to me.

With that being said, I knew she would be especially strict with me because I'm a girl. Unfortunately, being a young girl out at night always opens up the possibility of being exposed to danger in some way, and of course, my mom's concerns for my safety are valid.

My mom and I have conflicts regarding curfews because I think she is being unreasonable based on the circumstances. Typically, when I'm out at night, I'm with friends and we are in a familiar location. We are always aware of our surroundings and the people in our surroundings as well.

My mom's fear of the unknown can result in many calls and texts as the night goes on, but this can be frustrating for me when she already has my phone's location and has been informed of an approximate time that I will be home. I don't necessarily see her concerns as a lack of trust, but that she underestimates my level of responsibility and awareness when I go out at night. I always come home at the time we discussed, and if it gets to be a little later, I make sure to let her know.

Figuring out curfews used to be a lot more complicated when I first started going out at night with friends, but over time I have shown my level of responsibility and gained my mom's trust, so she has become more lenient with me (thankfully!), and I feel more relaxed when I get out of the house and spend time with my friends.

PG-13

ACT 3 - SCENE 1

BRINGING IT TOGETHER

NARRATOR

Start the conversation

Use these conversation starters to understand where both of you stand on the topic of curfews.

Daughter to Mom

- What concerns you when I am out at night?
- What safety rules are most important to you?
- Do you see any red flags with my friends?

Mom to Daughter

- What tools/knowledge would you use to deal with dangerous situations at night?
- Do you feel comfortable enough to call me if you need help?
- If not, why?
- What protocols should be followed if a curfew is in jeopardy?

III - MONEY & SPENDING

ARUNA AND KAAMYA KRISHNAN

MONEY & SPENDING

ACT 1 - SCENE 1

30 YEARS AGO

Mom talks about her family's modest beginnings and how that influenced her spending habits.

MOM

My parents did not grow up with a lot of money. My mom grew up in a village in India. My dad, as the first-born son, had to help provide for the family as early as his teen years.

Their humble backgrounds instilled humility. They passed this core value down to me and my brother.

My dad was the sole breadwinner in our family, so we had to make smart decisions around money. I did not have a weekly allowance or anything of that sort. If I needed or wanted anything, I had to ask my parents. That controlled any need to spend money. "Spend on what you need" was a mantra I lived by. The only non-essential spending I did on occasion was for toys or games - something for entertainment. Hey, kids need to have fun too!

I didn't feel deprived by any means, but I learned the value of money very early.

ACT 1 - SCENE 2

THE WORLDLY VIEW

NARRATOR

Financial Planners on one side help people save for retirement, college funds, and so on. With an almost equal and opposite force, we have many companies enabling and contributing to consumerism by way of products. Some we need, most we do not!

Another prevalent spending issue is the desire to buy things we cannot afford. Credit cards and the misuse of them has resulted in so many people having credit card debt. In March 2020, creditcards.com reported that 120 million people currently had credit card debt. Two big reasons they cited were emotional spending and unaffordable medical costs.

Emotional spending is something that affects people from teenagers to retirees. Constant ads in your face and the ease of purchase only propagate and magnify this problem.

Do you find yourself giving in to emotional spending?

ACT 2 - SCENE 1

TODAY

Mom talks about how the availability of too much stuff makes it harder (a constant battle) to teach kids restraint in spending.

MOM

As a parent, I want to make sure my kids have a sense of financial responsibility. I am not an excessive spender so I lead by example and reinforce good behaviors.

It's a lot easier to negotiate with a toddler than a teen when it comes to spending. With a toddler, a simple "You have too many toys" or "If you do this, I will get you that" gives the parent the final say in what happens.

With teens, the same approach should theoretically work, but dealing with them is a little more complex. Teens can be opinionated and often feel the need to defy their parents as a sign of individuality. This can create disagreement around what is a necessary purchase vs. unjustified or emotional spending.

I work with my daughter to track her spending and have her adhere to a budget to help her make wiser choices. This way the illusion of a limitless money tree gets corrected and the value of each dollar is better appreciated.

ACT 2 - SCENE 2

Daughter talks about her habits and lessons surrounding spending.

DAUGHTER

As a teen, money seems to be everything. As soon as I started to find a sense of freedom as a teenager, I realized that I needed money to do the things I wanted to do (whether it was with friends or by myself).

The struggle of trying to find part-time jobs that would hire me limited my access to money.

> "Hey Mom, can I go out and get some food with my friends?"
>
> "Yes."
>
> "I need money though."

This is a common conversation in our household, as I'm sure it is in others.

When it comes to spending, I am aware that I can't buy everything I like. Online window shopping is a favorite pastime of mine because it doesn't allow for excessive spending. In reality, it's not fair to my parents to continually ask for money, so I can say that I know my limits. Money isn't unlimited, and many teenagers may have a misconception that if their parents keep making money, they can keep taking money. If I don't have my own source of income as a teenager, then making a dent in the income of the adults in my life isn't the best way to go about it.

Spending money also means saving money, and I know that. As a teenager, you have to find the cheapest ways to have fun most of the time. I remember when I was younger, my mom would take me shopping and say, "Go to the sale section first." I was so confused at the time, but I went with it. She taught me how to calculate 60% off an item so quickly that I thought she was a math genius. Trust me when I say I still use that calculation trick in math class.

I definitely make unnecessary purchases and convince myself that I need certain things when, in reality, saving money instead of spending it (unnecessarily) will benefit me in the long run.

ACT 3 - SCENE 1

BRINGING IT TOGETHER

NARRATOR

Start the conversation

Use these conversation starters to understand where both of you stand on the topic of money and spending.

Daughter to Mom

- How much can we/I afford to spend per month?
- What can I do to help to earn some money for chores?
- If I get a job, can I use that for my personal spending?

Mom to Daughter

- What are the essential purchases (needs) that should be accounted for?
- Are there coupons or bargains that can be used for purchases?
- Can purchases wait for another month?
- Why is it important to make that purchase?

IV - SCREEN TIME

ARUNA AND KAAMYA KRISHNAN

SCREEN TIME

ACT 1 - SCENE 1

30 YEARS AGO

Mom talks about life in Africa and the limited programming on TV and how that enabled self-regulation of screen time.

MOM

I grew up with one TV station. Programming started at 4 pm and ended by 10 pm. Computers were available mostly for businesses. Movies came in the form of VHS tapes. The internet or streaming programming didn't exist.

In some ways, this was heaven! It was a built-in regulation to limit screen time. I don't remember my parents needing to set limits either. There was one central TV so they also had full knowledge of what I was watching and when.

This naturally encouraged activities like reading, playing outdoors, and hanging out with friends. All healthy outlets for growing children.

ACT 1 - SCENE 2

THE WORLDLY VIEW

NARRATOR

With the major advancement in technology, information is literally at our fingertips:

- The Internet
- 24 x 7 TV
- Smart Phones
- Tablets, Laptops, and Personal Computers
- Gaming Devices
- Social Media outlets

In 2019, the results of a study suggested that teens spent around seven hours per day on a screen. This was over and above any time they used for their schoolwork!

This has created a lot of new challenges.

- Less physical activity
- Less social interaction
- Cyberbullying
- Online predators
- Addiction to phones
- A decline in overall teen mental health

To address this issue, many health organizations are trying to put together suggested guidelines as to screen time by age for children. Parents are also taking responsibility for monitoring the time and content of screen time for their kids to make sure that they have a balance of entertainment, education, and non-screen activities that involve creativity or social interactions.

ACT 2 - SCENE 1

TODAY

Mom touches on challenges with defining screen time limits for teens and the importance of interpersonal interactions.

MOM

When my kids were young, I was their screen time police. My main rules were:

- Age-appropriate content
- Limited time spent on TV or tech
- More family time with reading, puzzles, and games
- Outdoor play to get fresh air and sunlight

It is a lot easier to set these guidelines for younger kids. Once they reach puberty, it gets a little more difficult. As a parent, my conflict has been around:

- How much decision-making to give them around deciding the right amount of screen time.
- How to substitute virtual interactions with social (in-person) interactions.
- How to reduce addiction and their submission to FOMO (Fear Of Missing Out).

I make sure my daughter is interacting with the right people and content by having an open conversation with her. Initially, I was a part of her social media network but as she's gotten older, I've removed myself from that web. I trust her to make good choices.

With all age groups, there must be a balance of tech vs. non-tech activity to maintain mental and physical health. I often remind my daughter to have some screen-free activities like reading, taking a walk, doing something creative, or going out with friends. Tech should help our lives, not BE our lives!

ACT 2 - SCENE 2

Daughter talks about how screen time can reduce productivity, energy levels, and the ability to get a good night's sleep.

DAUGHTER

Growing up in the digital age has allowed me to witness the rapid expansion of screens and social media. VHS tapes turned into streaming services, box TVs turned into flat screens, and flip phones turned into iPhones.

The ability to access videos, games, and music at any time of day seems like a little kid's dream! I loved using my screens when I was younger. Now, having so much access to information is intimidating and can be damaging.

Non-essential technology such as phones, laptops, and TVs often take over the day, distracting me from work, sleep, or other hobbies. When I sit around on my screen, scrolling for eternity, I'm unproductive and less likely to interact with people in real life. My energy levels are lower too.

My mom has always held me accountable for my screen use, making sure I put my phone away when doing work or getting rid of screens when it's time to go to bed. I can admit that as I've gotten older, my screen time has increased. It can be hard to self-regulate when there are so many different types of content and resources to explore. I think once you're able to recognize when screen time is too much, that same time can be devoted to more productive, self-fulfilling activities.

ACT 3 - SCENE 1

BRINGING IT TOGETHER

NARRATOR

Start the conversation

Use these conversation starters to understand where both of you stand on the topic of screen time.

Daughter to Mom

- What do you think is a reasonable amount of screen time per day?
- Do you have specific concerns about screen time?

Mom to Daughter

- Can screen time be regulated using designated time blocks for non-school-related usage?
- What other activities can we use to supplement screen time as a form of entertainment?

V - CLOTHING

ARUNA AND KAAMYA KRISHNAN

CLOTHING

ACT 1 - SCENE 1

30 YEARS AGO

Mom talks about how she was restricted in terms of defining a personal style.

MOM

Admittedly, I was not much of a fashionista growing up. For the most part, my mom bought my clothes. As a teenager, I started to have some opinions on what I wanted to wear, but it had to meet parental, cultural, and societal standards to some extent. Not that I wanted to dress provocatively, but the general guideline was to not draw attention to myself from the Indian community. My parents were trying to protect me from gossip.

With that, I did not have much latitude on defining my sense of fashion. Additionally, school uniforms were a norm.

Makeup was not allowed in school. It was more about blending in rather than standing out.

Botswana was not exactly a fashion capital of the world back then so there wasn't an endless number of fashionable options available. People did their clothes shopping in two or three key stores which meant there was a very good chance that a few of my classmates or friends would have the same dress or outfit I bought. Especially if the price had been discounted.

ACT 1 - SCENE 2

THE WORLDLY VIEW

NARRATOR

Culturally, clothing represents tradition and heritage. The fabrics and materials used for jewelry hold some meaning because it's passed down from the ancestors of that community. This can be seen in the various parts of Africa and India for example.

In the modern and western world, clothing can define:

- **Who you are**. Your individual style.
- **How you want to be perceived**. Classy vs. Not.
- **Your status**. Rich vs. Not.

With the rise of consumerism and technology, innumerable stores and choices for clothing exist. Some stores purely have an online presence. Consumers have become comfortable with shopping without the "touch and feel" experience. Worst case, they can return something if it doesn't meet their expectations.

The abundance of choices provides:

- Options in price
- Options in style
- Options in brand

Although some moms are guilty of falling for the brand hype, teens more easily get sucked into this trap. Teen celebrities and their promotional Instagram and TikTok accounts are BIG influencers of teen fashion and clothing choices and set the trends for this demographic.

ACT 2 - SCENE 1

TODAY

Mom credits her daughter for being fashion savvy and talks about how this talent should be handled with responsibility.

MOM

From a very young age, my daughter was quite opinionated about what she wanted to wear. I think she was two years old to be exact! It was very funny to watch a toddler care so much about how she wanted to put together her outfit for the day.

Little did I know that she had an innate sense of fashion. She takes pride in dressing well. Because of this, I like to consult with her when shopping. She has a great sense of what looks good and what items pair well.

As a mom, my main concerns around clothing are:

- Excessive spending. Is a piece of clothing worth the retail price?
- Drawing the wrong kind of attention. Finding the right balance between fashionable and edgy.
- The definition of enough. Being able to recognize the line between enough and excessive.

Bottom line, clothing has become a point for the teen to learn responsibility. The choices they make around what they buy and how much they buy are an exercise in decision-making. These are the things I encourage my daughter to think about:

- How much can she afford to spend?
- Do the clothes project an image of her that is true to her authentic self?
- Is there a need to add to her existing inventory of clothing?

If she can honestly answer the questions above, she is more likely to make good choices as a teen. As a mom, I like to see my daughter define her personal sense of style because it ties into defining her true self (instead of being a replica of some teen celebrity).

ACT 2 - SCENE 2

Daughter explains how clothing can be a statement and how trends can negatively influence naive teens.

DAUGHTER

Choosing what to wear when I was younger was my favorite part of each day. My initial passion for fashion was simply fueled by the opportunity to mix and match my clothes and use dressing up every day as a creative outlet. As I've grown up, clothing and fashion have become a very significant part of my life. I value fashion as an art form, and beyond that, I value fashion as a form of self-expression.

Some days I might wear darker colors with lots of layers, while other days I'll opt for smaller tops and brighter colors. I may choose an outfit inspired by current trends, historical inspiration, or just choose from whatever clothing happens to be clean that day. But clothing often depends on my mood. I find this is a common theme with kids my age; oftentimes the things we wear on the outside can be a reflection of who we are on the inside (your mood or personality). It's always important to be mindful of what clothing we wear based on the circumstance, but if an outfit is a true expression of style and personality, teenagers should get that creative liberty.

I used to be keen on keeping up with all the rapid trends, but in recent years I've taken a step back and chosen a more sustainable approach to my wardrobe. I make it a point to only seek out clothing I know I will wear for a long time. I used to claim, "Dad, I have nothing to wear!" and use that as an excuse to buy something new (and I will be the first to admit this is not a good excuse). As my mom mentioned, excessive spending is a potential issue when it comes to clothing. Rather than buying new things, I do my best to work with what I have, and I have learned to distinguish between clothing wants vs. needs.

Teenagers should have fun with fashion and use these developing years as a time to explore different facets of their personal style so they can feel as confident as possible in the clothing they wear.

ACT 3 - SCENE 1
BRINGING IT TOGETHER

NARRATOR

Start the conversation

Use these conversation starters to understand where both of you stand on the topic of clothing.

Daughter to Mom

- What is the budget for clothing spending?
- What would be considered unacceptable clothing styles?

Mom to Daughter

- What inspires your wardrobe selection?
- Do you get peer pressure around how you dress?
- Do you have something you'd call your personal style?
- When do you know it's time to add something new to your wardrobe?

VI - AFTER HIGH SCHOOL

AFTER HIGH SCHOOL

ACT 1 - SCENE 1

30 YEARS AGO

Mom shares the downside to her accelerated high school journey.

MOM

I was 15 years old when I graduated from high school. I skipped a few grades along the way and wrote a private exam to get my high school completion certificate (GED equivalent). Needless to say, I wasn't making a whole lot of decisions about my future or career at that time. I was too young, sheltered, and naive. There may have been other teens who were clearer on their goals and ambitions, but I was not one of them.

The most common and mainstream path after high school was a college degree. That was the path I followed, and I graduated with a Bachelor of Business.

- Did I know what a Business degree entailed? Not really.
- Did I know what all my career options would be with the degree? Not really.
- Did I understand the practical application of classes like Statistics or Economics? Not really.

The education system back then was more theoretical than practical. It was more about grasping the concepts enough to pass the exam. In retrospect, being a 15-year-old in college was a disadvantage. I did learn, don't get me wrong, but my lack of maturity prevented me from putting the lessons in context to hone in on my exact strengths and interests.

ACT 1 - SCENE 2

THE WORLDLY VIEW

NARRATOR

Today we have examples of people who have had significant success without a college degree - Steve Jobs, Bill Gates, and Mark Zuckerberg for starters. Each of them dropped out of college and went on to build successful businesses and unforgettable brands - Apple, Microsoft, and Facebook.

A college degree can set you up for a career in any field of choice whether it is the Arts, Business, Science, or anything else. The default path after college is to work *for* a company. Job Fairs are held in colleges to recruit these graduates. For students who have not been entertaining entrepreneurship, the corporate route is a no-brainer.

With the advancement of technology, there has been a shift in mindset towards possible career options. The ability to select specific online courses provides more flexibility and less financial burden to get the skills needed for either a traditional job or entrepreneurship.

The main factor that determines the direction is financial resources, the right network, and support. The security of a traditional job and the risk averseness of individuals make them hesitant to go the entrepreneur route. The middle ground tends to be in the side hustle where there is security and a chance to build a business at the same time.

ACT 2 - SCENE 1

TODAY

Mom talks through the evolution of her thought process around corporate vs. entrepreneurship.

MOM

After 15+ years in a corporate technology job, I've started exploring my entrepreneurial journey. As a management consultant, author, and podcaster, there are so many things I am learning.

- Defining my ideal client
- Defining my product/services
- Growing my customer base
- Marketing my products/services
- Building my network
- Serving my client

These things are also done in a corporate environment to help grow the business, but employees may only be involved with one or two of those aspects. Our experience gets us focused on specific disciplines and not the entire product lifecycle.

My daughter has a strong desire to be an entrepreneur. Looking back on my career, I wish I had started on the entrepreneurial path sooner. But that prospect always scared me because it felt too risky. Having stepped into that space, my horizons and knowledge have broadened. My recent venture has put me in a good position to understand and support my daughter if she wants to pursue entrepreneurship. Had I not tried this myself, I would have been less open to the possibility. The risk element of starting a business would have scared me and I may not have been comfortable with her career aspirations. The point here is about listening, keeping an open mind, and educating yourself enough to support your teen's choices.

ACT 2 - SCENE 2

Daughter shares her views on college and career.

DAUGHTER

I've always planned on pursuing higher education after high school. But believe me, there were moments where I questioned if it was worth it. In the world we live in, a 15-second video on TikTok can change the entire course of your life and career. With the rise of internet fame and the influencer culture, a majority of my generation doesn't seem to value the traditional path to "success." What defines success anymore? Why should some people work all their lives for a lifestyle that some can acquire overnight? I can definitely sympathize with this perspective of not wanting to work or take the college route. I've felt it myself too many times. The college route can often feel like the only safe route to take to guarantee a path to a well-earning career.

I saw it happen with my own mom: she worked hard at her corporate jobs for years, but it wasn't necessarily what she was passionate about. Only when she started writing books, making podcasts, and developing her business did I truly realize that there is not one path to take or one career to have. I tend to put pressure on myself, as do many other young adults, to have a plan and eyes set on a specific career. That pressure often surmounted my passions and planted seeds of doubt in my heart as I went through the college application process. I didn't know if I needed more time before college to 'figure things out', but I ultimately decided that college can be a tool for me to find what I'm passionate about and explore those interests in an environment of like-minded people.

I believe there is no direct formula for a successful career. I'd much rather take years to figure out what I like and what makes me happy than settle for something that feels mediocre because I was scared to take a risk. Choosing a path after high school does not mean you are choosing the path for your entire life!

ACT 3 - SCENE 1

BRINGING IT TOGETHER

NARRATOR

Start the conversation

Use these conversation starters to understand where both of you stand on the topic of life after high school.

Daughter to Mom

- What do you think is your best path after high school?
- What are the implications of various choices e.g. financials and job prospects?
- What are their pros and cons?

Mom to Daughter

- What do you consider your true passion and strength?
- Do you know people on this path that we can talk to?
- Would you like me to help you find someone?

VII - COMMUNICATION

COMMUNICATION

ACT 1 - SCENE 1

30 YEARS AGO

Mom discusses the parenting style that prevailed through her teen years.

MOM

I grew up in a time when parenting gave more emphasis to the voice of the parent. In other words, communication was mostly one-way - from parent to child.

There was not too much open conversation about the day-to-day happenings of a child. The focus tended to be very narrow and pertained mostly to basic needs and wants. Parents cared for their kids, as they do today, but the dynamic was not one of active and open engagement.

This prevented me from being open with my parents. I was never sure how they might react. I didn't feel I could confide in them or ask for advice. In retrospect, they would have liked for me to have a more open relationship with them, but somehow the precedent was never set that way.

PG-13

ACT 1 - SCENE 2

THE WORLDLY VIEW

NARRATOR

Broadly speaking, there are two camps of parenting today - old school and new school.

Old school, a.k.a. "Authoritarian" style includes helicopter, hover, and lawnmower parenting. All these forms of authoritarian parenting include an excessive (and obsessive) amount of parental involvement and decision-making. Parents get too involved in all aspects of the child's activities, solve all issues for them, and need to monitor their kids constantly.

This comes with its advantages and disadvantages. The main disadvantage is that the child doesn't grow their ability to work through problems at an early age. The sheltered approach can be detrimental when they finally step out of the house after high school because they haven't experienced life, and its potential pitfalls.

The new school approach, also called "Authoritative" style, involves more empowerment and creates a stronger parent-child relationship. Kids are given boundaries, but enough leeway to explore life and its consequences. This style of parenting has a prerequisite of trust. The child trusts they can be open with their parents and vice-versa. Otherwise, this approach can go totally awry.

ACT 2 - SCENE 1

TODAY

Mom talks about how her parenting style evolved with her kids' developmental phases.

MOM

When my kids were younger, I totally used the old-school approach. I wanted to be in control. I wanted my kids to be disciplined. I was the decision-maker. I think that was probably appropriate when they were young because that's when you can set the tone on acceptable behavior and related consequences. A five-year-old is a lot easier to discipline than a thirteen-year-old!

As my kids approached the tween years, I realized very quickly the old approach was not going to work for me or them! I am so glad for that timely realization. I chose to be more of a guide to my children rather than the enforcer of all things.

This has been a huge positive in terms of openness with my kids, especially my daughter. We can talk about a lot of things. We can disagree, have a discussion, and come to a final decision. Sometimes that involves compromise on my end, sometimes on hers, and sometimes both.

Knowing that my kids are not afraid of me and can come to me for anything is a real win for me as a parent!

ACT 2 - SCENE 2

Daughter talks about how the lines of communication opened up with her mom.

DAUGHTER

My mom mentions having a timely realization around my tween years. Well, so did I. I realized I was going through many different changes physically, mentally, emotionally, and socially. The fundamental aspect of any relationship is communication. I was often reluctant at that age to reach out to my mother for fear of judgment or a simple lack of understanding. We both grew up in completely different environments and I thought she wouldn't get it. Times are different now. I thought I was on my own. I used to think I was alone in my struggles, as teenagers tend to do. The angst that came from trying to figure out my identity led to conflict with my parents because I felt unheard.

It wasn't until my mom opened up a dialogue with me that I began to realize she had similar struggles as a teen and that communicating with her could help to put my thoughts and feelings into perspective. Of course, communication goes both ways. When my mom opened up about her life experiences and the lessons she's learned through them, I was more willing to open up to her.

When she listens to me today, her responses are filled with empathy, understanding, and validation. I emulate that same behavior when she comes to me. She doesn't belittle me because I'm the child. Instead, she listens to my opinions and we both leave a conversation feeling better and wiser than before. I even go to her with the silly, superficial things of everyday life and she comes to me. That fear of judgment has completely dissipated...I just had to give it time.

Cultivating healthy communication with one another meant checking in on each other, trusting each other, problem-solving together, and venting when we need to. The feeling of relief that comes with finding a safe space to share your emotions is worth any anxieties that may surface in your mind before reaching out.

PG-13

ACT 3 - SCENE 1

BRINGING IT TOGETHER

NARRATOR

Start the conversation

Use these conversation starters to understand where both of you stand on the topic of communication.

Daughter to Mom

- Are there any topics you feel uncomfortable talking about?
- Are there any current teen topics you'd like to learn more about?
- What were some of the challenges you faced as a teen?

Mom to Daughter

- Are there any topics you are curious about?
- Have you been going through anything you'd like to share?
- Is there anything in the relationship that you'd (like to) change?

VIII - SOCIAL MEDIA

ARUNA AND KAAMYA KRISHNAN

SOCIAL MEDIA

ACT 1 - SCENE 1

30 YEARS AGO

Mom remembers life before Social Media.

MOM

Guess what? There was no social media or email 30 years ago! My parents had it so easy. The primary forms of communication where I lived were phone calls, letters, or telegrams.

This was the age of film and physical photo albums. There were no risks around kids sharing too much about themselves with absolute strangers. Some teens did things behind their parents' back, but they were still more protected in that their "reach" was pretty limited.

I was very unadventurous. I was your typical goody-two-shoes. My parents had visibility into almost everything I did so they never had to worry. The environment at the time made it very easy not to get unwanted attention or divulge too much.

ACT 1 - SCENE 2

THE WORLDLY VIEW

NARRATOR

Social media has progressed from a photo-sharing medium to a total game changer! Businesses, communities, identities, and careers are launched on these platforms. There is a whole industry that caters to boosting your social media presence. Visibility is everything these days. Content creation is another industry that has gotten a major boost due to social media. There is no lack of videos, posts, or memes on social media. This is the minimum requirement for anyone who wants to promote themselves or their businesses.

Where there are pros, there are cons. The biggest downsides to social media are cyberbullying, attracting negative attention, and enabling data to be collected on your behavior and preferences.

"If you are not paying for it, you are the product" is a quote that has been used often in the context of social media. It was also recently referenced in Netflix's "Social Dilemma" documentary which talks about the perils of social media and provides a glimpse into the algorithms that capture a user's choices, posts, and interactions. We must all make a choice on how much harvesting of information we can tolerate. The negative light that has been cast on social media (and big tech) companies has forced them to give more weight to ethics around their policies and procedures.

ACT 2 - SCENE 1

TODAY

Mom shares how she was skeptical about using social media at first and how she handled her daughter's interest in joining social media.

MOM

I resisted Facebook and LinkedIn when they first launched. It felt like a very scary prospect. I liked being invisible. Eventually, I got on LinkedIn to search for jobs. Today, as a podcaster and author, I use LinkedIn and Twitter to promote my work. This is my primary use of social media.

My daughter has a couple of social media outlets. The primary requirement I had when she first got social media was that I needed visibility to her posts since she was younger. As a teen, she is sensible in what she posts and doesn't overdo the posting. From what I have observed, the feedback on her posts is healthy. When I got off Instagram, I was confident that she would continue to make good and smart choices in what she posted. She enthusiastically shows me all the photos since I no longer can electronically "like" her posts.

Building trust early is important. It comes down to communication with your teen. Being aware of what they are doing, feeling, and experiencing is crucial. We may not know 100% what they are saying and doing, so we need to equip them with information to make good choices when we are not around.

ACT 2 - SCENE 2

Daughter talks about the impact of social media influencers on teens and their sense of individuality.

DAUGHTER

I remember practically begging my dad to let me get an Instagram account when I was 11 years old. In hindsight, that was way too young! What was an 11-year-old doing on social media you ask? I wasn't doing much besides posting random photos of things in my bedroom and following my favorite Disney Channel celebrities. I didn't even know half of what was out there on the Internet, thanks to restrictions on screens when I was young. Social media was something new and exciting for kids my age, but it has evolved into something completely different today.

Social media is a huge part of teenagers' everyday existence. Call me guilty! I know plenty of people that are addicted to it. The ability to communicate quickly, share highlights from your life, learn about your interests, and become entertained are all reasons why social media is so prevalent in my generation. But it can come at a cost if you're not mindful.

There is so much information out there that it can become overwhelming. It's so easy to get wrapped up in the echo chamber that is social media. For example, following influencers who all look the same can lead to negative comparisons and issues with self-image. Too much screen time can take away from other responsibilities, and the ability to form your own thoughts and opinions can be stifled when you are constantly consuming the thoughts of others, even if it's not consciously. When I noticed my social media usage was bordering on unhealthy, I started implementing social media breaks. It's important to remember that you aren't missing out on much. Everything is so hyper-curated that the line between reality and what's on your screen can be blurred.

My mom mentions her concerns about attracting negative attention which I understand. But this aspect can be easily avoided. If you are mindful about your posts and use common sense about the image you are creating for yourself, there shouldn't be a problem.

ACT 3 - SCENE 1

BRINGING IT TOGETHER

NARRATOR

Start the conversation

Use these conversation starters to understand where both of you stand on the topic of social media.

Daughter to Mom

- What scares you the most about social media?
- What are the things you'd be comfortable with me sharing?
- Are there some things that you'd say are no-nos?

Mom to Daughter

- Do you have any concerns with the responses you receive?
- What are some of your favorite pages?
- Do you feel restless/tired after being on social media?
- How much time do you spend?
- What makes you stop using it?

IX - MENTAL WELL-BEING

MENTAL WELL-BEING

ACT 1 - SCENE 1

30 YEARS AGO

Mom reflects on the attitude toward mental health when she was an adolescent.

MOM

From a cultural standpoint, where I grew up, mental health was not an openly discussed topic. I don't even think there was awareness of the exact meaning of mental health. Even if there was in the medical circles, the common folk were not talking about this much. Seeing therapists or psychiatrists was considered only for those people who had "lost their minds". People were very ignorant about the benefits of this branch of science.

Many women suffered, in silence, from depression their whole life. Since their husbands didn't understand mental health or have the resources to learn, they were nothing more than bystanders... not realizing that their wives could benefit from professional help!

Kids, however, had a more carefree environment. There wasn't constant pressure from preschool to be independent. That allowed kids to have some level of emotional and social maturity before taking on real responsibilities.

As a teenager, I did not experience too much stress or pressure in high school. Generally, there was a feeling of abundance in choices whether it was colleges or courses. It wasn't the rat race that seems to exist today. As a result, anxiety and depression weren't as prevalent among teenagers. Coming from a less privileged background, I perceived any opportunity I could gain as positive.

ACT 1 - SCENE 2

THE WORLDLY VIEW

NARRATOR

The *Stress in America 2020 Report* published by the American Psychological Association stated that the effects of the pandemic caused a national mental health crisis. It expressed concerns about how this would eventually play out in terms of social and health perspectives.

The report calls out stress factors such as:

- Financial disruption
- Uncertainty about the future
- School disruption
- Discrimination
- The election

A 2020 CDC report stated, "During late June, 40% of U.S. adults reported struggling with mental health or substance abuse."

With the prevalence of all this information and the reporting of mental health issues, more people now have the courage to talk about it. Teens, in particular, were reported to have increased cases of anxiety and depression compared to past years. This unfortunately resulted in more suicides in some instances. In other cases, teens were able to talk to their parents and get help in the form of a life coach, adopting a healthy lifestyle, and/or medication.

These problems continue to persist due to limited social interactions, overuse of social media, and loss of loved ones during the pandemic.

If you or someone you know is struggling or in crisis, help is available. Call or text the National Suicide Prevention Lifeline at 988 or chat 988lifeline.org

ACT 2 - SCENE 1

TODAY

Mom shares her thoughts on supporting her daughter through the stressful period of high school and the road to college.

MOM

It is a tough period for teenagers right now. Aside from the stresses of being teens whose brain development favors impulse over rationality, they must deal with a pandemic, college applications, and all the uncertainty around these things.

I really empathize with teens. My daughter has also been dealing with anxiety and depression. It's been a tough journey and we've had to take it a day at a time. It took me a little longer than I would've liked to recognize her symptoms. It's sometimes easy to miss when it is layered on top of the typical hormonal changes of teens.

She had been questioning her feelings in silence for a few years and just didn't feel comfortable coming to me because she thought there was something wrong with *her*. When she finally opened up about what she was feeling, I remember saying, "This sounds like depression." We went to see her doctor within a few days and found her a therapist shortly thereafter. That has helped her to learn about herself and find ways to cope and become more resilient.

As a mom, I see it as my responsibility to be there for my daughter. It is such a delicate period in life. I want to provide an environment for her where she feels safe. Safe to talk to me about issues. Safe to share her feelings. Safe from criticism.

Teens need our support right now. They may not have the mental maturity to put things in perspective since their experiences are limited and tend to give them a flawed sense of reality. As parents, we must reinforce the fact that this situation will pass, with time, and we will be able to move along even if it means an altered future.

ACT 2 - SCENE 2

Daughter shares her personal experience with mental health and how she would like to see more open dialogue around the topic.

DAUGHTER

Today, mental health is a lot more openly discussed and recognized, especially among teens. My friends and I talk about our mental health frequently and we speak vulnerably.

My hope and greatest wish for the future is for mental illness to be discussed without the stigma. The stigma surrounding mental health and treatment can be perpetuated by loved ones or relatives who are unwilling to advocate for mental health when someone they know is struggling. That stigma can prevent people from getting the proper support they need.

I've been learning to cope with depression and anxiety for most of my teenage years. Countless stressors loom over the heads of teenagers right now, including school, friendships, self-esteem, and the future. Coping with mental illness has been an uphill battle, but with a trustworthy support system, it's become a lot easier. Reaching out for help is never something to be ashamed of. I've had to educate not only myself but also my family members on mental health and the importance of having conversations surrounding mental well-being.

Mental illness can be extremely debilitating; it can affect everyday life and relationships. Teenagers may invalidate their own emotions because it's easier to ignore their struggles than get the help they need. They may fear invalidation or judgment from those closest to them. These were habits I had before I just went for it: I opened up the conversation with my mom and I told her that I needed help. And I got it. What a huge relief to feel heard! At the end of the day, my mother cares about my well-being and I thought she wouldn't understand what I was going through until she expressed her own struggles with mental health.

Although there is still progress to be made in many families, schools, and in the greater conversation, it's important to remember that everyone is fighting their own battles, whether it's obvious on the surface or not. It starts with self-awareness which then can lend itself to better emotional intelligence and a renewed control over your mind.

It can be so hard to suffer in silence. Although it sounds cliche, you are never going through it alone. Opening up this conversation about mental well-being can lead to less shame or resentment toward ourselves and better empathy toward others. We are unified by our shared fears, anxieties, and emotions.

ACT 3 - SCENE 1

BRINGING IT TOGETHER

NARRATOR

Start the conversation

Use these conversation starters to understand where both of you stand on the topic of mental well-being.

Daughter to Mom

- Do you know anyone who has had depression?
- What symptoms/behaviors did they display?
- Where can we learn more about mental health (in teens)?

Mom to Daughter

- How are school and your social life?
- Are there things/thoughts that bother you on a daily basis?
- What activities bring you joy?
- Do you have a close friend?

X - SOCIAL LIFE

SOCIAL LIFE

ACT 1 - SCENE 1

30 YEARS AGO

Mom talks about the limited scope of her social life as a teen.

MOM

When I think back to being a teen living in Botswana, I remember the simplicity of life. Hanging out with my friends, walking to the mall, and having sleepovers were the main components of our social lives.

In high school, our parties had a few recurring themes:

- No boys
- Dancing
- Good food

In most cases, there was a parent around hosting the parties so there wasn't an opportunity for something to go awry. All my friends were grounded and there was no curiosity to do anything that could get us into trouble.

Having a core group of friends with similar values made us close and we could share our thoughts and feelings openly. We were each other's support system.

Another aspect of my social life was at the community level. We celebrated Indian cultural events, festivals, and religious ceremonies. This brought Indians together to celebrate our heritage and keep us grounded in our traditions and roots.

PG-13

ACT 1 - SCENE 2

THE WORLDLY VIEW

NARRATOR

Social life is a key part of today's High School experience.

Some of the in-built opportunities are:

- Prom
- Homecoming
- Band and Orchestra events
- Football games
- Other high school sports events

This allows students to socialize within the context of their school and classmates. These are relatively controlled events in that there is some form of supervision or monitoring.

The students themselves define additional social activity outside of school. Some of the choices may include:

- Lunch/Dinner with friends
- Trips to the mall or thrift stores
- Sleepovers
- Dating
- Parties

Each of these requires high schoolers to exercise judgment. Although the first two are relatively harmless, the last three can come with consequences. Drug use, sexual assault, and teen pregnancies are some of the grave consequences which can affect physical and mental well-being. The key decision for teens to make is around *who* they choose to surround themselves with. Sometimes well-intentioned kids get caught in the web of poor choices and become a casualty of that circumstance.

The pressures of high school combined with the lack of a good support system have led many teens to commit suicide. A 2019 study by the CDC states that about 19% of teens in the previous year thought about suicide, and 9% committed suicide.

Teens today have so much more to deal with. It is key that parents are tuned in to their activities and build that relationship of trust. This provides a safe environment for the teen to confide in their parents and ask for advice rather than seeking acceptance from friends that could lead them down the wrong path.

*If you or someone you know is struggling or in crisis, help is available. Call or text the National Suicide Prevention Lifeline at 988 or chat 988lifeline.org

ACT 2 - SCENE 1

TODAY

Mom talks about how social life can be a catalyst for growth and maturity.

MOM

My high school years were uneventful. A limited friend circle and a somewhat curated environment created a sheltered social life for me.

In retrospect, I realize this hindered my growth from a social and emotional standpoint. I did not have the opportunity to deal with difficult people or situations. This was a drawback.

Because of my experience, I recognized how important it was for my kids to have some element of social life to create balance in their lives and also to teach them how to deal with unfavorable circumstances.

I see value in the "live and learn" philosophy with some qualifications:

- I am aware of my teens' circle of friends and can identify red flags early
- I know their general itinerary and can ensure their safety
- I assure them they can come to me for help on anything

Mutual trust starts to create accountability within the teen. If teens make mistakes, they can have a dialogue with their parents to come to a resolution and use that experience to guide the future. We all learn from our mistakes. Teens should have enough space to make choices and evaluate the outcomes of those choices. As long as they know they can go to their parents, teens can experience life and learn how to be responsible.

ACT 2 - SCENE 2

Daughter discusses the need to be more selective about friendships and the value of spending time alone to reflect.

DAUGHTER

I grew up with a small circle of friends that I would hang out with frequently. But, naturally, as time goes on things change. People grow apart and friend circles may diminish. When I reached high school, I didn't necessarily have a "friend group" but rather a selection of friends that I could hang out with for different reasons. I didn't like cliques and only hung out with people that made me feel good.

I attended football games, school dances, and parties but never truly enjoyed them. It was conformity that got the better of me. I wanted to fit in, which meant putting myself in scenarios I didn't necessarily want to be in. My FOMO (Fear Of Missing Out) often got the better of me. Once I realized that I was doing myself a disservice by spending time around others who brought my energy down, I had a significant breakthrough. Why should I sacrifice my identity and wants for the sake of others? Why should I care about the opinions of people who I barely know?

I was able to seek out social experiences that truly gratified me following this epiphany. I said no to things I didn't want to do and yes to things that excited me.

My mom (and the restrictions of the pandemic) helped me come to this realization. Spending time with myself and a few close friends was so much more fulfilling. Quality over quantity. When my circle got smaller, my mom trusted me to go out and come back home feeling good about myself and my friend circle. Again, communication about what I was up to helped free up limits on my social life.

PG-13

ACT 3 - SCENE 1
BRINGING IT TOGETHER

NARRATOR

Start the conversation

Use these conversation starters to understand where both of you stand on the topic of social life.

Daughter to Mom

- Are there social activities you are not comfortable with?
- What concerns do you have, if any, about my friends?

Mom to Daughter

- How do your friends make you feel?
- How do your friends support you?
- What do you enjoy doing with them?

EPILOGUE

NARRATOR

As we've seen, people's experiences and environments form their opinions. Opinions don't have to be static. The only way to get through to others with opposing or conflicting views is through communication. Rational, and unemotional communication. Keeping conversations on an even keel prevents unnecessary defensiveness and promotes better listening. By having dialogue, the two parties can either find the middle ground or be willing to shift their original stance.

MOM

Although I have a good relationship and open line of communication with my daughter, putting this book together really enabled me to understand things from her perspective. I was able to peel back one more layer of the onion and understand how a teenager thinks. Even though I was a teenager, the problems and needs in those times were different.

The book also gave us a way to collaborate in such a way that we learned more about each other in the process. That is what I hope for the moms and their daughters who read this book.

DAUGHTER

Working on this book meant quite a lot of reflection and introspection. Being able to see my own mother's point of view and her experiences regarding different topics unlocked even more empathy and respect than I had for her before.

My hope with this book is that other teenage daughters like me can view their relationship with their mothers in a more positive light. Although fostering better communication and finding common ground with one another might be hard at first, time will lead to successful results if both parties are willing to put in the work for the sake of each other's well-being and the future of the relationship.

CLOSING CREDITS

By Aruna Krishnan

To my daughter - This book is extra special to me because I was able to collaborate with my daughter. Your ideas, feedback, and enthusiasm for quality really elevated this book. Thank you, Kaamya!

To my book launch crew - Charitha Seemakurthi, Sasidhar Nagapatla, Robb Conlon, Walter Gainer II, Vidya Raghu, Uma Achutha, Josh Kangley, Bhuvana Raju, Ashok Pattabiraman, Reena Bassi, Zarine Shahid, Ally Bubb, Uma Chandra, Ganesh Babhu, Janet Sharbuno, Nancy Kalsow, Kevin Wondra. Thank you so much for your support!

By Kaamya Krishnan

To my mother - I'm so grateful that you encouraged me to work on this passion project with you. You've taught me how to become a better writer, leader, and woman in the process. You've shown me that it's never too late to chase your dreams. I'm so proud of you! I don't say it enough. Thank you, Mom!

To my father and big brother - Your unwavering support means the world to me! Thank you for the advice, wisdom, and laughs when I need it. You keep me inspired and motivated. Thank you, Dad and Karan!

ABOUT THE AUTHORS

ABOUT THE AUTHORS

ARUNA KRISHNAN

Aruna Krishnan is a Tech Leader, Author, and Podcast Host. Her *Busy Mind* book series covers competencies such as Emotional Intelligence, Problem Solving, and Leadership. She discusses these topics with simplicity, providing readers with an easy way to apply the lessons and frameworks provided.

Her interest in mindfulness coupled with her experience as an Information Technology leader has led her to write books that demonstrate new and simple ways of thinking about age-old problems.

Aruna has been featured in Authority Magazine, Thrive Global, and WomLEAD. In 2021, WomELLE magazine named her one of the Top 25 Women to follow for Women's History Month.

She is an advocate for Mental Health and Women's Empowerment. Her main mission in life is to give people hope and help them find happiness through a process of self-discovery. She does this through content, stories, and inspiration!

She can be reached at:

LinkedIn - www.linkedin.com/in/aruna-krishnan2022

Twitter - @LeadThatThing

KAAMYA KRISHNAN

Kaamya Krishnan is a student at New York University pursuing entertainment, media, and journalism. Her interest in emotional intelligence and interpersonal relationships has led her to pursue writing as a way to share her unique perspectives.

She wrote her first book *PG-13: A Guide to Strengthening the Mother-Daughter Bond* to illustrate her experiences with her mother and convey how communication is important for the success of a relationship. She hopes to help other mothers and daughters communicate effectively, navigate conflict, and find common ground through their shared experiences.

Kaamya's mission in life is to open up greater conversations regarding mental health, diversity, and social consciousness through different forms of media.

She can be reached at:

Linkedin - www.linkedin.com/in/kaamyakrishnan

Instagram - @kaamyakrishnan

OTHER BOOKS BY ARUNA KRISHNAN

Visit Amazon's Aruna Krishnan Page

EMPOWERING WOMEN
LISTEN TO LEAD THAT THING!
A Podcast By Aruna Krishnan

Available on **Google Podcasts**, **Apple Podcasts**, and **Spotify**

A NOTE FROM THE AUTHORS

Thank you for taking the time to read our book. We would greatly appreciate it if you would leave us an honest review on Goodreads and Amazon.

www.ingramcontent.com/pod-product-compliance
Lightning Source LLC
Chambersburg PA
CBHW020434220526
45464CB00002B/699